Red Texas

Road Trips

By ALLAN C. KIMBALL

Great Texas Line Press
Fort Worth, Texas

Texas Redneck Road Trips

*for bulk sales
and wholesale inquiries
contact*
**Great Texas Line Press
Post Office Box 11105
Fort Worth, TX 76110
greattexas@hotmail.com
www.greattexasline.com
800-73TEXAS**

★ Editor: Amy Culbertson
★ Book Design: Allan C. Kimball
★ Front Cover Photo: Allan C. Kimball
★ Title Page Photo: Madonna Kimball
★ Back Cover Photos: (right) Madonna Kimball,
   (top left) Fort Worth Convention & Visitors Bureau,
   (lower left) Barry Shlachter.
★ Interior Photos by Allan C. Kimball unless otherwise credited.

DEDICATION: Many thanks to Barry Shlachter.

CONTENTS

INTRODUCTION

OK, Bubba, I know what you're thinking: "So what's a redneck road trip anyways?"

It'd be easy to answer that it's a road trip rednecks take, but then you'd ask what I think a redneck is. So I'll answer both.

First off, a few statistics with which you'll be able to knock the socks off your cousins in foreign lands like Louisiana. Texas has 268,580 square miles. Now that's as large as all of Connecticut, Delaware, the District of Columbia, Maine, Maryland, Massachusetts, New Hampshire, New Jersey, New York, Pennsylvania, Ohio, Rhode Island, Vermont and West Virginia combined[1]. Combined, my friend. Texas has 254 counties and one[2] of them alone is larger than Connecticut. Seven are larger than Delaware. Fifteen are larger than the state of Rhode Island and 40 are about the same size as that teeny little state, but that's nothing — we've got a *park*[3] about the same size as Rhode Island.

The point of all this is that Texas is big. And with all that space it has lots of places that'll just blow your hat in the creek. Amusement parks and art museums and sophisticated resorts, places like those, seem to get all the travel-related ink these days, but this book is about the unusual places that real people go to have a little fun.

The road-trip destinations in this book are often off the beaten track, often surprising in some fashion, often unusual — and always, always entertaining and worth the trip. These are places you'll be telling stories about for months, maybe years. These are places you don't have to get dressed up for. Flip-flops or hunting boots, gimme cap or cowboy hat, tank top or *Texans* T-shirt, torn jeans or plaid Bermudas are just fine. You can laugh out loud in these places. You can wave howdy to other folks, smile, and they'll actually smile and wave back.

And that's what a redneck is, really, just someone who waves at strangers and someone who waves back. A redneck is just someone who left pretentions back at third grade recess, just a person not afraid of a little hard work every now and then, just a person looked down on by grouchy sociology teachers and people who live in Manhattan, just someone who wants to enjoy the moment and have a little fun.

No, you don't have to be someone with a glorious lack of sophistication to be a redneck. You just have to understand way deep down inside your soul that sophistication doesn't really matter at all. To mangle up some Shakespeare: Be not afraid of being redneck: some are born redneck, some achieve redneck, and some have redneckedness thrust upon 'em.

Take a road trip or two and you'll have more fun than a lost dog in a meat market. So tap into your inner redneck and partner up with your favorite nagivator[4] and go ahead on down the road with this book. Ain't nothing to be afraid of but snakes and dry counties.

~ *Allan C. Kimball*

Notes

Mentioning Shakespeare and providing footnotes makes this book officially a scholarly work so that snobs don't have to be afraid to be seen reading it. And don't worry, this is the last time we'll do either.

[1] Combined area of those northeastern states is 265,248 square miles.

[2] Texas' Brewster County has 6,193 square miles; Connecticut has 5,544.

[3] Big Bend National Park has 1,252 square miles; add in nearby Big Bend Ranch State Park's 422 and you get a total of 1,674 square miles. Rhode Island has 1,545.

[4] That's the person in charge of reading maps and constantly telling the driver where to go.

Alamo Heights
TOILET SEAT ART MUSEUM

Sit down and let me tell you a story about a retired master plumber with a fixation on a bathroom fixture. The result? The Toilet Seat Art Museum. Yes, a museum filled to overflowing with lowly toilet seats — more than a thousand of them. But you don't sit on these. Barney Smith has created collages on the lids, seats and backs. Who else do you know who has a toilet seat with an 11-point rack? After a hunting coup with his father, Barney decided to put the deer antlers on a spare seat. Then he started doing the same thing with all sorts of other junk. He glues artifacts and photographs in place, carves art and signatures into the pressed-wood seats.

He got the idea for turning all this into a museum after a customer at a garage sale told him all those collages were true art. A local TV station came out and filmed him; then network and syndicated television crews showed up, along with writers for magazines and books.

It takes him about 20 hours to make up one of his seats. Now he's got 45 years' worth of them. Among his artworks are a seat with $1 million in shredded cash from the Federal Reserve Bank, a piece of the Challenger shuttle, a model train set and Saddam Hussein's Iraqi palace toilet.

FYI: 239 Abiso Avenue, Alamo Heights, 210-824-7791. *Note:* Call first. The museum is in Barney's garage, and he's not always home.

Barney Smith loves to show off his toilet seat collection.

Eat all this food in one hour and you get it free.
Main photo courtesy of Big Texan Steakhouse.

Amarillo
BIG TEXAN STEAK HOUSE

Eat a 72-ounce steak and all the fixin's and you get it free. You know you can do it. After 20 ounces you hope you can do it. After 48 ounces you doubt you can do it; then you're just looking for a place to puke it all up with a smile on your face, 'cause you know you'll have a story to tell your buddies for years to come. You might need a gallon or so of antacid if you succeed.

This is so appropriate because, after all, Amarillo is the beef capital of the world. The food challenge takes place on a raised platform in the middle of the restaurant, so you can be the main attraction. About 89,000 have tried; about 8,500 have triumphed. One was a 64-year-old grandma.

The restaurant looks like every saloon you've ever seen in Western movies, except this is way bigger, of course. The wait staff dresses up as cowboys and cowgirls. The walls are covered with Western art, cowboy artifacts like branding irons and lariats, lots of stuffed animal heads and animal horns. You might even hear "Amarillo by Morning" playing while you try to scarf down one of these top-notch steaks.

The restaurant has a huge Texana and Route 66 gift shop. And you'll find the Big Texan Motel next door, so you don't have to go far to rest after you've pigged out. Er ... beefed out.

FYI: www.bigtexan.com, 7701 E. I-40 (exit 75), Amarillo, 806-372-6000.

This'll beat all you ever stepped in: old Cadillacs stuck nose-down in the dirt in the middle of nowhere and covered with graffiti.

Local millionaire Stanley Marsh 3 (he didn't cotton to Roman numerals) thought this up in 1974 and got it built by the Ant Farm, a group of art hippies from San Francisco. He wanted a piece of public art that would baffle all his neighbors. It worked. The Caddies are supposedly sticking up at the same angle as the Great Pyramid of Giza, and visitors are encouraged to spray-paint their own remarks or art on the old cars. Take a picture, because the next dude will spray paint over your beautimous artwork.

Decades have passed. The Cadillacs have now been in the ground as art longer than they were on the road as cars. Stanley might've been a few bricks shy of a load, but now Cadillac Ranch is a major attraction up here where the birds build their nests out of barbed wire. You can spend hours in this desolate field pondering the philosophical implications. Hunh? Exactly.

Think Caddies are too good for you? Then head on down the road to nearby Conway and the Slug Bug Ranch to contemplate five Volkswagens nose-down in the dirt.

FYI: Cadillac Ranch, exit 60 on the south side of I-40 west of Amarillo. Slug Bug Ranch, exit 96 on the south side of I-40 east of Amarillo near Conway.

No one knows why Cadillac Ranch (top), west of Amarillo on I-40, was built. The newer Slug Bug Ranch (bottom), east of Amarillo on I-40, is surrounded in the same mystery.

Gigantic Cowboys Stadium (top). In addition to football games, the stadium also hosts concerts. *Photo by Diana Woodall.*

Arlington
COWBOYS STADIUM

You live, eat, sleep and crap Cowboy, so you have to visit Cowboys Stadium. It's the kind of thing God might've built if he had the money — a playspace so huge you'll get a week-long neck crick from staring at it.

How huge is it? Well, it's the largest domed structure in the world, with 3 million square feet and a capacity of up to 100,000 fans. The column-free room stretches for a quarter-mile, so you could even hold drag races inside — and somebody probably will, at some point. And of course it has a big roof that can be open or closed.

Founded in 1960, the Cowboys have won five Super Bowls ... but you knew that. Only thing better than watching them Cowboys may be the Frito pies you get at the concession stands.

Thing is, you can enjoy more than football in this place. For example, it hosts concerts with folks just up your alley, like Kenny Chesney and Tim McGraw. It's OK that the stage is so far off, because the stadium boasts a 160-by-72-foot video screen that's 90 feet above the floor.

The concourses aren't just that usual gray concrete you see in most stadiums either. You're going to find classy art all over the place.

And they do tours.

FYI: www.dallascowboys.com, 900 E. Randol Mill Road, Arlington 76011, 817-892-4161.

Sure, Austin is the hippie-dippie capital of Texas, but you gotta love a guy who builds a monument to junk in his backyard. It towers above you, about 80 twisting tons of golf clubs, roof vents, tires, car parts, dive gear, surfboards, air-conditioning ducts, hair dryers, mirrors, trophies, shoes, hubcaps, bicycles, tools, road and street signs, license plates — more stuff than you could possibly count even if you used all the fingers and toes of all your rugrats. One wall is made of bottles. Another of crutches. A stairway of tires with concrete-art centers takes you up and inside the Cathedral to a meditation room.

Vince Hannemann started this in 1989, and it's become famous; he estimates about 10,000 visitors a year stop by to ooh and ah and laugh. This artistic junkpile has even hosted weddings and birthday parties.

Why? Vince says he just started off playing, like building a treehouse or a fort out of blankets when you were a kid. It's a place where he can live out his fantasies.

Vince looks over the twisting pile, getting a wistful look and a sparkle in his eye, and then says quietly, "It makes me smile." It'll make you and yourn smile, too.

FYI: 4422 Lareina Drive, Austin, 512-299-7413
Note: The Cathedral of Junk has no set visiting hours, so call Vince to make certain he's home.

Just one view of the imposing Cathedral of Junk.
Photo by Madonna Kimball.

Katie Hall, 10, and Bryson Soria, 8, riding through the woods at Crooked Creek Cycle Park.

The whole family gets to rattle some bones and breathe in exhaust fumes at this here dirt-bike park.

Lori and David Royalty opened CCCP in 2002 on 504 acres, with 24 miles of family-friendly trails rated from very easy to moderately difficult, all quite twisty and interesting.

David knows his business; he started riding when he was 7 years old.

These trails are for motorcycles and four-wheelers only — three of them are bikes only. And all the trails are one-way, making them much safer to scoot around.

You'll find beautiful trails ranging from 1.8 miles to 8 miles in length, with names like Twist & Shout, Hog Wild, Bonehead, Bertha and Lost in the Woods. Heavily wooded, bordering creeks and a lake, these trails are pretty enough to rival many state park trails.

Pay attention to the trail markers: You don't want to get lost in the woods, and a skeleton riding a motorcycle along the trail will remind you of that. Sometimes, birds will make nests in the skeleton's skull, making him a true bird-brain.

And don't miss Big Bertha's underwear at the end of the Bertha Trail.

FYI: www.crookedcreekcyclepark.com, 4730 T.K. Parkway (FM 939), Axtell 76624, 940-367-3917.

How cool is this? Stuffed bobcats, Judge Roy Bean's gavel, a goat with two faces and a shrunken head.

Welcome to the Frontier Times Museum. It's not anything like the places they made you go on school field trips. Look around and you'll see money from all over the world, saddles, pioneer stuff. There's melted glass and cement from a building destroyed by the A-bomb dropped on Nagasaki at the end of World War II, a *McGuffey's Eclectic Reader* and an 1867 chalk slate, antique books and Bibles and toys and perfume bottles.

But wait; there's more. Here's a Venetian birthing chair. There's a fireplace encrusted with fossil shells, a stereopticon, an old hair curler set that looks like a torture device. Here's a dugout canoe and old firearms, arrowheads, moccasins and bows. There's even a map of Texas made of rattlesnake rattles.

In back is the Texas Heroes Hall of Honor, which includes Texas Ranger Joaquin Jackson, actor/artist Buck Taylor, pioneer scout Jose Policarpo Rodriguez, writer J. Frank Dobie, rancher Maudeen Marks and country singer/songwriter/saloon owner Arkey Blue.

And don't miss the piece everyone talks about: the shrunken head of an 18-year-old Jivaro Indian woman.

FYI: www.frontiertimesmuseum.org, 510 13th Street, Bandera 78003, 830-796-3864.

Now, be honest, have you ever seen a bona fide human shrunken head before?

Visitors like 6-year-old Ella Pryor can swim with the gators or just hang out and look at them. *Photos by Madonna Kimball.*

Did you used to wrassle gators in grade school? If not, this is the place to get up close and personal with a congregation of alligators — and do it safely.

No, this ain't the Florida rock band, this is an alligator rescue and adventure park where you can swim with alligators. Real ones. When they brag about "hands-on interactions," they aren't kidding. And you can get face-to-face with more than gators. Let the guides introduce you to crocodiles, caimans, snakes and tortoises. You can feed the alligators, take pictures with reptiles, swim with the gators and get educated at one of the big shows. Meet Big Al — at 13 feet 4 inches long, he's the largest alligator in captivity, they say. Don't miss Banana, the 14.5-foot python.

Alligators were once an endangered species, but they were removed from the list in 1985, and they've made a hell of a comeback. In the Gator Country area alone, you could find about a quarter of a million of them these days. In Texas, gators now roam from the Rio Grande to the Red River.

Gator Country is the home sanctuary of Gary Saurage, the alligator rescuer and conservationist who has starred in TV shows on the CMT, Animal Planet and A&E channels.

If you get hungry, you can eat out at the Gator Country Café overlooking the park.

FYI: www.gatorrescue.com, 21159 FM 365 (I-10 exit

Cabela's ain't for sissy outdorks. It's a redneck cathedral, filled to overflowing with everything you really want for Christmas or your birthday.

One of the most impressive things inside Cabela's isn't for sale — it's a large aquarium full of game fish at the base of a three-story hill populated with taxidermied critters.

The hill is there to make you want to graze over at the fishing tackle display or the gun cabinets to find just the right tools to get your own fish and wild critters. Or scope out a bass boat or kayak or an ATV and all sorts of accessories for your boat or pickup or four-wheeler, to make bagging and toting your prizes all that much easier.

And of course you have to dress the part, so you'll find all sorts of clothing — men's and women's — from full camo to rainwear to boots and shoes. Even jammies.

Shooting games will help you educate Bubba Junior.

Wander upstairs, and in one area you'll find packaged goodies like jars of jerky, brownies and mouth-watering butter pretzels. In another area is outdoor stuff that'll help you hang out at the deer lease in comfort. And when all this shopping raises your appetite, just head over to the café.

It probably won't surprise you to learn that Cabela's is one of the top tourist attractions in the state.

FYI: www.cabelas.com, 15570 I-35, Buda 78610, 512-295-1100.

Cabela's features a hill full of stuffed critters and the tools to take some of your own. *Photos courtesy of Cabela's.*

Shoppers can spend days checking out all the goodies along 15 miles of shopping trails at First Monday.

CANTON
FIRST MONDAY TRADE DAYS

This is a flea market so big they need several days to fit "Monday" in. Big? Oh, yeah. How about 300 acres and more than 4,500 vendors. Gives "shop till you drop" new meaning.

So what, you ask, can you find here? You'll find lots of jewelry and Mexican imports and antiques and clothing, but you expected that. How about trunks and trash cans? Navajo pottery? Face paint? Mounted longhorns, skulls and horn furniture? Honey straws, candy and soap? Pet tag engraving, collars and leashes? Cowhide rugs and steak brands?

If you'd like something special for your significant other, you can find a booth where you can get anything you want embroidered while you shop around.

Want to put your own little personal casino in your garage? A couple of booths will supply you with old slot machines, dice games and other casino supplies.

You know how the wife has been bugging you about getting some classy lawn flamingos? Find all sorts of flamingo items right here.

Plenty of food booths and restaurants, too.

You can even take concealed-handgun classes here.

The main thing to remember is when First Monday is open — Thursday through Sunday before the first Monday of the month. But it's not open on Mondays.

FYI: www.firstmondaycanton.com, 800 Flea Market Road, Canton 75103, 903-567-6556.

Eddie Fonseca seems to smile all the time. You would, too, if you owned a place called Frank's Bait and Taco. That's right — vittles for your tummy now and bait to catch some catfish later.

It's impossible not to smile at this roadside café near Canyon Lake. Yes, they sell tacos and lots of other foods like hot dogs and enchiladas. Yes, they sell bait — after all, a huge lake is just down the highway. No, they don't sell the bait inside the restaurant; it's sold in a shack on the side. No, Eddie's name isn't Frank. It's complicated. Ask him.

Look around. You'll see donated items like pirate flags and signs and caps, model ships, a portrait of Hill Country legend Hondo Crouch, fish, cups, seashells, collectible plates, paddles, samurai swords, ship wheels, model cars, fishing rods, art nouveau prints and a Venezuelan spear dating from 1932 that nearly killed the father of a customer.

Don't miss the rubber chicken by the door to the bait house. It's all decked out in pirate gear, complete with eye patch. You'll even find funky stuff in the restrooms, like the "Santa Stops Here" sign by the men's commode.

All this in a place where you can get breakfast tacos all day long — except at breakfast time (they don't open until 11 a.m.).

FYI: 20115 Farm Road 306, Canyon Lake 78133, 830-223-7036.

You won't find an inch of Frank's that's not covered with some piece of donated memorabilia or kitsch (top). *Photo by Madonna Kimball.* **Owners Frenchy and Eddie Fonseca.**

A Tex Ritter statue welcomes visitors to the Texas Country Music Hall of Fame; inside, several displays feature items belonging to the Western star. *Top photo by Madonna Kimball.*

TEX RITTER MUSEUM &
TEXAS COUNTRY MUSIC HALL OF FAME

If you don't know who Tex Ritter is, ask your father. Or grandfather. He was one of the most popular Western singers and movie stars a few decades ago. But I'll bet you do remember "Do Not Forsake Me," his biggest hit.

This museum honors Woodward Maurice Ritter, born in 1907 in nearby Murvaul. It was started by Tommie Ritter Smith, who wanted a Tex Ritter museum because her father and Tex were first cousins and she had lots of Ritter memorabilia. John Ritter, Tex's son, donated more items. You know John from TV's *Three's Company*.

The museum then expanded to include the Texas Country Music Hall of Fame, with exhibits on each inductee. It's redneck blues heaven.

One wing is Tex's, including clothing, albums, hats and photos, and one display case features John.

One area is like a 1950s malt shop, complete with an old jukebox playing the music of the inductees. Above the booth is the TCM Disc Jockey Wall of Fame with photos.

You'll also find the old control room of radio station KGRI in Henderson, where another local legend, singer Jim Reeves, once worked as a DJ. Reeves has a life-size memorial statue at his grave, three miles east of town on U.S. 79.

FYI: www.carthagetexas.com/halloffame, 310 W. Panola, Carthage 75633, 903-694-9561.

Oh, heavenly hosts! Right here are doughnuts to die for, honey buns that melt in your mouth, snickerdoodles to keep the rugrats quiet and cinnamon rolls bigger than your fist.

Honestly, these baked goods are so good, they'll make your tongue jump out and lick the eyebrows off your head.

Since 1974, the bakery has been baking all the above, along with apple fritters, a vast assortment of breads, coffeecakes, cookies, croissants, Danish, long johns, muffins, pies, stollen, strudels, tortillas and turnovers. And those cookies are something special — every imaginable flavor and size, including special ones for the various holidays. Some come with an icing so sweet they'll melt your teeth if you eat too many of them.

A word about the doughnuts is in order. Their plain cake doughnuts are not the mushy, tasteless lumps you find everywhere else. These are Old World doughnuts that are dense, crusty and tastier than any you've ever had before. Whatever you do, don't buy fewer than half-a-dozen, because after you eat one you'll want more-more-more.

They even do wedding cakes — "with Flavor," they proclaim. And that's the thing at Haby's: Everything is chock full o' flavor. And peek back at the kitchen. It's the cleanest you've ever seen.

FYI: www.habysbakery.com, 207 U.S. 90 E, Castroville 78009, 830-931-2118.

Meghan Gass with a sampling of Haby's Bakery goodies.

All sorts of stuffed dead animals watch while you stuff
yourself with dead animals at Mikeska's.

JERRY MIKESKA'S BAR-B-Q

No redneck worth his gimme cap can resist good barbecue, and this place has all the other joints beat, not just because of the food, but because the place is stuffed to overflowing with stuffed critters — deer, bear, partridge, etc. That makes it the perfect barbecue joint — you can eat dead animals while being watched by dead animals.

Mikeska's has an edge on other barbecue joints by offering steaks in addition to the ribs and brisket and sausage. They've got chicken and fajita tacos, too. You can even get baked potatoes, a welcome rarity in the barbecue-joint business. And it's all tender and juicy and tasty.

If you want to tote some home, they also sell the meats by the pound, the sides by the pint or quart. They'll cater your special event, too.

The Mikeska clan has been dubbed "Texas' First Family of Barbecue," with food joints in other Central Texas locales, each featuring its own delicious barbecue recipes, as well as a mail-order business.

Jerry Mikeska, 80, still runs the Columbus operation, as he has since 1948.

In addition to all the stuffed critters on the walls are photos of Jerry with President George W. Bush, baseball legend Nolan Ryan, several Texas governors and Bum Phillips.

FYI: www.jerrymikeskas.com, 4053 U.S. 90 (I-10 exit 698), Columbus 78934, 979-732-3108, 800-524-7613.

CORPUS CHRISTI
ROLLER DERBY QUEENS

Maybe none of these ladies looks like Raquel Welch in *Kansas City Bomber*, but don't doubt that the women of the CC Maidens league are true roller derby queens. On derby nights, elbows fly, with lots of girl-on-girl action.

CC Maidens like Nasty Nelly, Sideshow Sally and the Bi-Polar Roller bring adrenaline-pumping, action-packed mayhem to roller derby the way it was meant to be.

The Maidens started up in 2010 and feature all the aforementioned stalwarts along with the Queen of Hurts, Olive Danger, Katy Scary and Nekromaniak. Some of these gals are smaller than a bar of soap after a week's wash, but they're all tougher than one-eared country cats. The president of the group is Bruja Loca Raquel Ramos, who looks so sweet sitting on the sidelines but can get just a tad frantic when she's on the rink.

They perform at different venues, but usually at the Ayers Event Center in Corpus Christi.

And they're not alone. Roller derby is making a big comeback; you can find leagues all around Texas, including clubs in Abilene, Beaumont, Dallas, Denton, El Paso, Longview, Odessa, San Antonio, Wichita Falls and many more. The best-named group is the Ann Richards Roller Girls in Austin — bet they've got big hair under their helmets.

FYI: To find a league near you, check out www.derbyroster.com.

The CC Maidens are the quickest and toughest gals on skates in Corpus Christi.

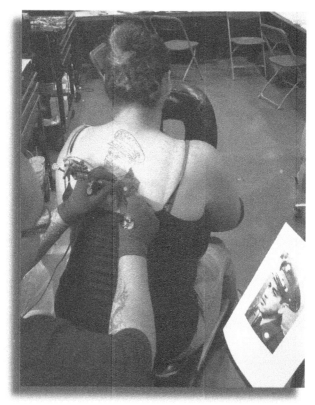

Artist Ron Perez tattoos an image of Jamie Colunga's grandfather Rudy Garza on her back. *Photo by Madonna Kimball.*

Sure, showing off your tattoos is fun, and scopin' out others can be even better, depending on the canvas they're on. Right here at this annual convention you'll see hundreds — heck, thousands — at a time.

Ron Urbanec and Susie Hughes of Skindustries Tattoos host the event. Vendors come in from as far away as California and Wyoming, bringing caps, inks, purses, candles, figurines, plugs and jewelry. You'll find all sorts of tattoo artists, henna tattoos, piercings, seminars, belly dancing, a Miss Tattoos by the Bay contest and more.

Except for old pirates and drunken sailors, you might think tattoos are a relatively contemporary fad. You'd be wrong. They were all the rage in ancient Egypt about 6,000 years ago. Remember that iceman they found frozen in the Alps after a couple millennia? He was covered in tats. If a 5,291-year-old dude can sport 57 tattoos, you probably can.

In 1891, Sam O'Reilly invented the tattoo machine, making the transfer process from concept to skin much easier and quicker. If you come up with a piece of custom art, you can find a tattoo artist who will bring it to life on your epidermis (see photo).

FYI: www.tattoosbythebay.com, 361-249-5270. If you don't want to wait for the convention, try Skindustries, www.skindustriestattoos.com, 10926 Leopard Street, Suite E, Corpus Christi 78410, 361-242-0603.

CORSICANA
LEFTY FRIZZELL
COUNTRY MUSIC MUSEUM

You gotta wonder why country singers don't dress up in those purty rhinestone suits like Lefty Frizzell did. At least Lefty's museum preserves his rhinestone-studded jackets and shirts, custom-made boots and music.

This place celebrates all that twangy music and pomaded hair you grew up on, in the town where William Orville Frizzell was born in 1928.

Lefty's best-known song was probably "Saginaw, Michigan," but his influence lives on in plenty of country stars who came after him. While you look, you can listen to his music, like "If You've Got the Money (I've Got the Time)."

The museum is run by the Navarro County Historical Society, which also runs the adjacent Pioneer Village, with its collection of 16 old buildings, a stagecoach and a mobile jail used to pick up rowdy rednecks back in the 1920s.

Some of the pioneer buildings date to 1840. Look for the stern visage of Dr. James Cooksey in one of them. Brrrr.

The buildings are furnished with period stuff. One displays real Confederate money, another shows various barbed wire, another an arrowhead collection.

Lots of Bonnie and Clyde memorabilia, too. Clyde Barrow was born just 26 miles away.

FYI: www.cityofcorsicana.com/pioneer-village, 912 W. Park Avenue, Corsicana 75110, 903-654-4846.

The Lefty Frizzell Museum (top) is adjacent to Pioneer Village, packed with old cabins, a stagecoach and artifacts.

Big Tex welcomes visitors to the State Fair of Texas.
Photo courtesy of the State Fair of Texas.

First off, you're greeted by Big Tex, who wears size-256 jeans, size-70 boots and a 75-gallon hat. Then you get to munch on an unimaginable variety of fried foods.

Among the recent fried-food offerings have been fried Coke, fried bubblegum, fried Samoas and Thin Mints, fried butter, fried cactus bites, fried jambalaya, fried bacon cinnamon rolls, fried chocolate tres leches cakes, fried pork wings, fried mac-and-cheese sliders and fried beer. What's not to like?

Once upon a time, notable fair-food fare was pretty much limited to the corny dogs that were invented here in 1942, but things have changed. In 2006, that fried Coca Cola got everyone talking. Since then, more and more outrageous fried delicacies have brought worldwide attention to a fair that began in 1886 as a livestock exhibition with horse races and pie contests.

The fair grew, ultimately leading to a new venue — today's Fair Park — and drawing in millions of people each year. It's routinely voted as the top event in all of Texas. Our little ole fair got so popular that in 1986 Fair Park was designated a National Historic Landmark.

Today, you can enjoy pickup truck exhibits, music, art, a cheerleading contest and a midway of games and rides.

FYI: www.bigtex.com, 3921 MLK Boulevard, Dallas 75210, 214-565-9931.

Poker and slots on a real Indian reservation. Wooo, doggies, it don't get much better than this.

If you're so poor you can't pay attention, maybe Lucky Eagle isn't the place for you. But if gambling is your only retirement plan, this is the only legal place to do it in Texas. Where else can you do all sorts of bad stuff — smoking, gambling, and drinking — at the same time on the same stool?

The casino is way out in the middle of noplace, on the Kickapoo Indian reservation on the banks of the Rio Grande, near Eagle Pass, which is already off from the rest of Texas.

Opened 1996, it's small as casinos go — nothing like the elaborate castles of hedonism that line the Las Vegas Strip — but it is the only one in Texas, so you can't be picky. It has a poker room and a bingo room, but it's mostly just slots — more than 1,800 of them. Notice they don't call them "slots," though, but "gaming machines," which are actually based on bingo. Those spinning reels and ringing bells are "for entertainment purposes only." The giveaway is that strange bingo card off to the lower left side of the screen.

The casino is working on an expansion that will include a hotel, so you won't have the inconvenience of driving a few miles away to lay your weary head down.

FYI: www.kickapooluckyeaglecasino.com, 794 Lucky Eagle Drive, Eagle Pass 78852, 888-255-8259.

Sure, you think you're playing slots and you look like you're playing slots, but you're actually playing bingo at the Lucky Eagle Casino (inset), the only legal casino in Texas so far.

Helicopter pilot Terry Honaker takes hunter Neill Woodward up to stalk feral hogs in West Texas.

Fort Stockton
PORK CHOPPERS

Shooting wild hogs is a passel of fun, but now you get to shoot 'em from the sky in a whirlybird.

More than 2 million feral hogs run around in Texas these days, and as of 2011 it became legal to hunt them from helicopters and shoot as many as you'd like.

Feral hogs do some $400 million in damages each year, destroying habitats of other animals, trampling crops, harming trees and wetlands, killing fawns and young lambs and goats, tearing up recreational areas and occasionally even terrorizing tourists in state and national parks.

Near Fort Stockton, Smith Helicopters is among a growing number of charter companies across Texas providing aerial support for hunters, farmers and ranchers wanting to eradicate feral hogs.

What's remarkable is how easy these hogs are to see from the air. While they may run and dart all over the place, there aren't many places for them to hide, and a helicopter can easily keep up with their pace. This makes the critters as easy to shoot as fish in a barrel for a decent marksman. It's so easy that being on a pursuit could be described as porn for hunters.

Feral hogs are unprotected, non-game animals, so they may be taken by any means at any time of year with no limits. You do, however, need a hunting license.

FYI: Terry Honaker, Smith Helicopters, 432-448-2168.

PAISANO PETE & SQUAWTEAT PEAK

Here's the world's largest roadrunner. He's 11 feet tall and 22 feet long. Of course, this is a statue, and it doesn't go "beep-beep," but it's a great place to take pictures of the kids and show your relatives back in Tennessee that things really are bigger in Texas.

And being big is all Pete does. He doesn't even have a little plaque to tell visitors that roadrunners (members of the cuckoo family) are rather prolific in these parts or that the name "paisano" is a Mexican Spanish slang word for the bird meaning, roughly, "little buddy." But he is big.

Pete was created out of fiberglass in 1980. There's also a museum and an old fort here, but it's Pete people remember.

You'll remember Squawteat Peak, too. It's a prominent cone-shaped hill rising about 300 feet from the desert. Yes, that's its real name. When they're in stock, you can buy a gimme cap, with the name and a drawing of the hill on it, from the Bakersfield (population 7) Exxon station.

Don't make fun of the peak. It's a relatively important archaeological site with remains of shelters built by prehistoric hunter-gatherers.

FYI: Paisano Pete is at the corner of Dickinson Boulevard and Railroad Avenue in Fort Stockton. Squawteat Peak is 34 miles east of town along I-10 in Bakersfield. Visitor Center: www.fortstockton.org, 1000 Railroad Avenue, Fort Stockton 79735, 432-336-2264.

Paisano Pete, one of the world's largest roadrunners (top) is in Fort Stockton. East of town on I-10 is Squawteat Peak.

**Fort Worth Stockyards National Historic District (top)
shows off longhorns twice daily.**
Photos courtesy Fort Worth Convention & Visitors Bureau.

FORT WORTH
REDNECK CAPITAL of TEXAS

Don't let the city's ballet and opera and zoo and classy museums fool you, this is the Redneck Capital of Texas. This is Cowtown; this is where the West begins.

It's called Cowtown because after the Civil War Fort Worth was a major livestock shipping and supply center, and it more than lives up to its name today.

First off, you've got the Historic Stockyards, filled with sites from the Old West, Texas-themed shopping and food, rodeos, Western saloons, museums and the Fort Worth Herd twice-daily cattle drive. You'll see legendary structures, such as the Livestock Exchange Building; the Stockyards Station shops and restaurants in the old sheep and hog barns; and numerous Western-wear shops on Exchange Avenue.

The Cowtown Coliseum in the Stockyards was home to the world's first indoor rodeo in 1918 and features rodeos almost every weekend these days.

And how about them cowboys? No, not the ones who play football down the road, but the ranch hands and rodeo riders who helped shape the history and legend of Texas. They're honored at the Cowboy Hall of Fame in the Stockyards and at the nearby Texas Rodeo Cowboy Hall of Fame.

Yes, two museums dedicated to cowboys. The emphasis here is on rodeo stars, but you'll also find other Texas legends, including baseball's Nolan Ryan, musician Willie Nelson and popular physician Dr. James "Red" Duke, who may wear the state's most famous cowboy hat. Look around them and you'll see all sorts of horse-drawn wagons used in ranching; footwear and photographs telling the story of Justin Boots; Chisholm Trail artifacts such as branding irons, maps and cowboy clothing; Amon Carter's long black Cadillac; and more. And kids wondering what life was like on an Old West cattle drive can pack and saddle a horse, learn about brands, stock a chuck wagon or dig in sawdust for arrowheads.

Don't forget the women. Over there is the National Cowgirl Museum and Hall of Fame, where you can get a video of yourself riding a mechanical bull.

Then you're going to want to visit the Texas Civil War Museum, because you know the South will rise again.

Way yonder is the Texas Motor Speedway, where you can snap your head around 4,762 times in a couple hours watching NASCAR and IndyCar racers go round and round and round. It's a 1.5-mile oval with 24 degrees of banking in the turns to help those racers go about as fast as they can. And in case you've consumed a little too much liquid refreshment, TMS has a unique counter that displays the laps counting both up and down. There's even a separate dirt track.

Top off the day with a night at Billy Bob's Texas, the world largest honky-tonk.

Unlike the typically tiny honky-tonk in your town, Billy Bob's is so huge it can squeeze 6,000 people inside at once. Legally. Plus room for polishing belt buckles with your sweetie when the band plays. You can get your Lone Star or Shiner at one of more than 32 bar stations.

National Cowgirl Hall of Fame. *Photo courtesy of NCHF.*

Twangy music is featured at Billy Bob's Texas.
Photo courtesy Fort Worth Convention & Visitors Bureau.

Before you start whining about the lack of a mechanical bull, notice that you can watch real bull riding every Friday and Saturday night in the indoor rodeo arena here.

Then stay the night at Miss Molly's, a former bordello where good-lookin' ghosts roam the hallways. Built in 1920, it's now a romantic bed-and-breakfast inn you won't forget. Just remember this caution on a sign inside: "Street ladies bringing in sailors must pay for room in advance."

And as befitting a redneck capital, Fort Worth has a Cabela's (see the Buda entry for details; all the stores are similar) where you're going to want to wander aimlessly.

FYI: www.fortworth.com, 817-336-8791. Billy Bob's: www.billybobstexas.com, 2520 Rodeo Plaza, 817-826-2340. Cabela's: www.cabelas.com, 12901 Cabela Drive, 817-337-2421. Cowtown Coliseum, www.cowtowncoliseum.com, 121 E. Exchange Avenue, 817-625-1025. Miss Molly's: www.missmollyshotel.com, 109 E. Exchange Avenue, 817-626-1522. National Cowgirl Museum: www.cowgirl.net, 1720 Gendy Street, 817-336-4475. Stockyards National Historic District, www.fortworthstockyards.org, 500 NE 23rd Street, 817-624-4741. Texas Civil War Museum: www.texascivilwarmuseum.com, 760 Jim Wright Freeway North, 817-246-2323. Texas Cowboy Hall of Fame: www.texascowboyhalloffame.org, 128 Exchange Avenue, 817-626-7131. Texas Rodeo Cowboy Hall of Fame: www.texasrodeocowboy.com, 121 E. Exchange Street, 817-624-7963. Texas Motor Speedway: www.texasmotorspeedway.com, 3545 Lone Star Circle, 817-215-8500.

Play cowboys and Indians with live ammunition at the Texican Rangers, a Cowboy Action Shooting (CAS) club on a historic working cattle ranch.

Each shooter adopts an alias appropriate to a character or profession of the late 19th century, a Hollywood Western star or a character from fiction, then develops a costume accordingly. Many participants enjoy the costuming aspect of the sport as much as or more than the shooting competition itself.

The Rangers have 14 stages — including a train and a fort, a mercantile and a homestead — furnished with individual scenarios and brief scripts so that each shooter is the star of his or her own mini-movie. Young and old, men and women, all have fun. They shoot at steel targets with Old-West-style weapons — revolvers, rifles and shotguns. The resulting "BANG-clink!" is addictive. You even get a badge.

Texas is a hotbed of CAS activity, with dozens of local clubs all over the state. If you were so inclined, you could shoot every weekend.

The sport is sanctioned by the Single Action Shooting Society, and participants now number more than 100,000 around the world.

FYI: www.texicanrangers.org, 210-316-0199. For information on a Cowboy Action Shooting club near you, visit www.sassnet.com.

Jeff Deskins (aka Kettleman, among Cowboy Action Shooters) takes out the steel bad guys at the Texican Rangers range.

U.S. Navy ball caps are among the thousands of authentic military surplus items found at Col. Bubbie's.

If your granny wore combat boots, she got them right here. Where do you start with Col. Bubbie's? This shop is so jammed with bona fide military-related goodies that they have to hang stuff from the rafters to pack it all in.

This was all Meyer Reiswerg's idea back in 1972. He promoted himself to colonel, wore raucous Hawaiian shirts and greeted everyone who walked in the door with a loud and happy, "What's going on, Bubbie?"

This is real military surplus. As you wander around the mothball-scented aisles, you'll spy radios, dogsleds, a .50-caliber machine gun. You'll find uniforms from various countries, military coffee cups, hundreds of military-themed T-shirts, 40-mm shell casings, Navy wardroom china, Israeli Air Force and Army T-shirts, backpacks, helmets and liners and covers, flags, boots, military ball caps, jackets, mess kits, pistol belts and holsters, ghillie suits, surgical masks, bandages, forceps and unused specimen bottles.

There's a T-shirt with Arabic writing on it that translates as "infidel" — you might wanna be careful where you wear that one. Don't miss the sign by the grenades: "Not recommended for airline travel."

The good colonel passed away in 2009, but wife Suzie carries on as commander-in-chief.

FYI: www.colbubbie.com, 2202 Strand, Galveston 77550, 409-762-7397.

THE CROSS OF OUR LORD JESUS CHRIST

This is the place to go on Sundays — Easter weekend, especially. You just can't drive by a 190-foot-tall cross.

The cross is completely unexpected as you drive along the empty ranges of I-40 east of Amarillo, but it's impossible to miss. You can see it for 20 miles off.

The cross is made of tubular steel covered with white galvaluminum panels and is one of the tallest crosses in the Western Hemisphere.

Steve Thomas and 100 workers of his Caprock engineering company fabricated it in 1995. He also paid for it. Steve, a member of Saint Vincent de Paul Catholic Church in Pampa, wanted to show his faith with a public symbol and found the site in Groom. The Diocese of Amarillo accepted the gift.

The Cross of Our Lord Jesus Christ is illuminated at night; according to Cross Ministries, which runs the site, it is seen by 10 million motorists on I-40 each year.

When you stop, you'll notice much more here than that giant cross. You'll see a Calvary hill with the three crosses; there are life-size Stations of the Cross surrounding the central cross. Off to one side of the property is a large building housing a religious jewelry shop and the Bible History Theater. In front of the theater is a Jesus Fountain, inviting even more photographs.

FYI: www.crossministries.net, exit 112 on the south side of I-40 E, Groom.

Groom's giant cross, surrounded by Stations of the Cross statues, surprises visitors along I-40.

Anthony Salisbury and one of his medium-sized, 80-pound, hand-caught catfish. *Photo by Brady Knowlton.*

GUN BARREL CITY
CATFISH NOODLING

Rednecks don't sit around and wait for fish to come to them; they go out in the river and get 'em. They stalk their game. Yes, since 2011 it's become legal in Texas to catch a catfish by hand.

You don't need no fancy fishing tackle or even jug lines, just your hand and a strong tolerance for pain.

Simple, really. Just reach under water and feel around in a nice big hole or under a big rock. Search slow and steady. It's all by feel, so you're essentially fishing blind. Be careful: These are also places where snakes, turtles and alligators like to hang out. Catch the catfish by the lip or put your hand down its gullet. And face it, either way, you're going to get bit. Love it or hate it, you won't forget it.

You can do this in most waterways around Texas, but Purtis Creek Lake, near Gun Barrel City, is quite a popular noodling spot, with its blue, channel and flathead catfish. The season runs from May through July and part of August.

FYI: Anthony Salisbury, www.handfishingtexas.com, 972-743-1712, offers "noodling adventures." If you prefer to catch catfish the usual way, contact North Texas Catfish Guide Service's Chad Ferguson at www.learntocatchcatfish.com, 817-522-3804; on Lake Lewisville, the catfish capital of Texas, Chad runs Rednecks Catfish Guide Service and makes Redneck Catfish Bait Soap, www.TxCatfishGuide.com, 817-306-0055.

BEER CAN HOUSE

Within two seconds of standing in awe in front of this place, you'll want to do the same to your house when you get back home, but in your heart you know all the metal in all those cans would tilt your trailer over to one side, and your current live-in wouldn't stand for that.

First thing you notice is the wind rustling through the beer can tops that form a curtain across the front of the house. All outside walls of the house and the adjacent visitor center (where the garage was) are completely covered with flattened beer cans.

Inside the cottage is mostly empty except for kitchen appliances and one room where a video history of the house plays. One wall inside has a curtain made of flattened Falstaff Centennial Edition beer cans with George Washington's portrait. A side fence is made of beer and soda cans, some flattened and some stacked in a wooden frame.

This was the brain fart of John M. Milkovisch, who died in 1988. He didn't want to waste his empty beer cans, so he just started putting them on the house. How many beer cans? Estimates range from 30,000 to 50,000.

John once said, "I don't consider this art. It's just a pastime. But sometime I lie awake at night trying to figure out why I do it."

FYI: www.beercanhouse.org, 222 Malone Street, Houston 77007, 713-926-6368.

A curtain of beer can tabs provides shade and music at Houston's Beer Can House..

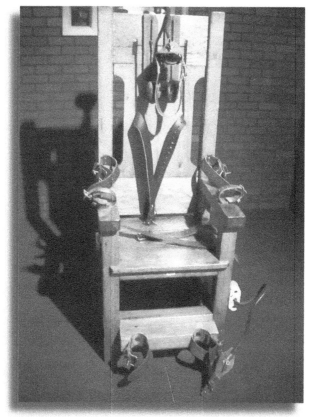

Ol' Sparky, once the state's electric chair for executions, is a star attraction at the Texas Prison Museum.

TEXAS PRISON MUSEUM

Relive those fond memories of your days in stir and bring home a bobblehead prisoner doll from the gift shop for the top of the TV.

The Texas Prison Museum is home to Ol' Sparky, the electric chair used to execute several prisoners before the switch to lethal injection. You can see syringes used in the lethal injections as well. And there's a display of items used protesting the death penalty.

You'll also see a chrome-plated, pearl-handled Colt .45 automatic pistol taken from the car that Bonnie and Clyde bought the farm in.

Displays include executed prisoners' last words and portraits, a history of the Texas Prison System, art made by inmates, guards' weapons, prisoners' balls and chains, a video and artifacts from the famed Texas Prison Rodeo, plus various items used in escape attempts, including a bicycle and a paper-and-cardboard revolver that looks amazingly real.

When it functioned as the state's primary lock-up, Huntsville Prison was a place no one wanted to go to. The exhibits here now educate the public on what real life behind bars is like, despite what you might see in films or on TV.

You can even sit in a 6-by-9-foot replica cell.

FYI: www.txprisonmuseum.org, 491 Texas 75 N., Huntsville 77320, 936-295-2155.

IRAAN
ALLEY OOP FANTASYLAND

Dinosaurs died out about 230 million years ago, so you may wonder what one is doing out in the wind-blown mesas of West Texas today.

The 72-acre Fantasyland Park is so far out in middle of nowhere in a town so small, there's almost no there there. But there is a tribute to venerable cartoon character Alley Oop and his sidekick Dinny.

Creator V.T. Hamlin got the idea while working as an oil-patch roughneck in the area in 1927. He saw truckloads of dinosaur bones the steam shovels and scrapers were digging up when they were preparing sites for wells and pumps.

Hamlin started drawing the caveman comic strip in 1932, preceding Fred Flintstone by a couple of decades. At its peak "Alley Oop" was carried by 800 newspapers. Today more than 600 papers carry it.

You might have even danced to the popular early-'60s song "Alley Oop."

Also located at the park is the Iraan Archaeological and Historical Museum, full of Native American and ranch artifacts and lots of fossils.

By the way, you pronounce the town's name "Ira-Ann," after Ira and Ann Yates, on whose ranch oil was discovered in the late '20s.

FYI: www.iraantx.com, Alley Oop Lane, Iraan 79744, 432-639-2232.

Fantasyland is home to both Dinny the Dinosaur and Alley Oop, famous in song and comic strip.

The Kemah Boardwalk will entertain you all day long.

Get sick on the amusement rides, pig out on shrimp, pet a stingray. High living.

You might think you're on Coney Island, but you're actually in the small town of Kemah, on Galveston Bay, about 20 miles from downtown Houston.

The boardwalk here opened in 2001, was devastated by Hurricane Ike in 2008 and then was rebuilt better than ever.

This is a family getaway. Saunter along the boardwalk itself and watch shrimp boats, sailboats and motor boats come and go. Check out the carnival games, a double-decker carousel, Ferris wheel, mini train, dancing fountains to watch or play in, and the Boardwalk Beast, a 96-foot-tall wooden roller coaster that has one vertical drop of 92 feet, with speeds of more than 50 mph and 42 crossovers (a record number for a wooden coaster). And it runs just five feet from the water's edge.

The Boardwalk FantaSea yacht will take you out for sightseeing or dinner cruises, or you can shop for toys, gifts and souvenirs.

The boardwalk has plenty of restaurants, including the Aquarium, where you dine surrounded by fish; after dinner you can go downstairs and pet the stingrays.

Special events include Mardi Gras and a beer festival.

FYI: www.kemahboardwalk.com, 215 Kipp Avenue, Kemah 77565, 877-285-3624.

Leakey
BIKER HEAVEN

Pronounced "LAY-key," this little Hill Country town is at the heart of the best motorcycle roads in Texas. Says who? Ride Texas magazine, almost every year.

Riding along Ranch Roads 337, 336 and 335 — a 100-mile loop of steep, twisty, gorgeous hills — you might also see giraffes, zebras, wallabies, camels and unusual deer, since this area is full of ranches stocked with exotic game.

The D'Rose Inn is the perfect place for riders to sleep — it caters only to motorcyclists and bicyclists. It has three rooms, 11 cabins, a pool, a pavilion, grills and picnic tables.

Nearby, the Hog Pen has kindred company along with barbecue and beer.

If you're in the mood for fried chicken, zip over to Chickin' Earl's. But make sure it's on a Tuesday, because that's the only day he's open.

The Frio Canyon Motorcycle Stop — like D'Rose and the Hog Pen — is owned by bikers. They stock their Stop with supplies of everything you'd want to find while on the road, and their Bent Rim Grill provides another oasis in the hills.

FYI: Chickin' Earl's: 703 U.S. 83, Leakey 78873, 830-232-5001. D'Rose Inn: www.droseinn.com, 5527 U.S. 83, 830-232-5246. Frio Canyon Motorcycle Stop: www.friocanyonmotorcyclestop.com, 657 RM 337 W., 830-232-6629. Hog Pen: www.thehogpenstore.com, 373 U.S. 83, 210-288-3995.

Bob the Wooden Motorcyle Man guides motorcyclists into Leakey's D'Rose Inn, which accommodates only bikers.

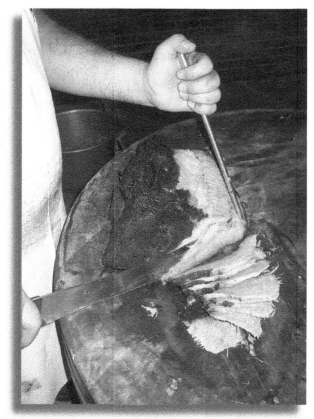

Carving up the brisket at Kreuz Market, one of four tasty barbecue joints in Lockhart.

Lockhart
BBQ CAPITAL OF TEXAS

The Texas Legislature declared Lockhart the Barbecue Capital of Texas, so it must be true. Find out for your own self at one — or better yet, all — of the four joints in town:

• Black's Barbecue bills itself as Texas' oldest barbecue spot continuously owned by same family (since 1932), but it's not the oldest in town. Also, it's not really "open 8 days a week" despite what the sign says. It just feels that way, owner Norma Black says.

• Chisholm Trail Bar-B-Que offers a large selection of salads and sides in addition to a variety of meats.

• Kreuz Market is the granddaddy of them all, opened in 1900, though its building is the newer, due to a move. You still can't get barbecue sauce or forks there, but anyone who has jalapeño cheese sausage on the menu isn't stodgy.

• Smitty's Market has been using the same pits for more than 75 years and still serves up brisket on butcher paper.

According to the City of Lockhart, 20,000 people eat barbecue in Lockhart each week — close to double the population of 13,633.

FYI: Black's: www.blacksbbq.com, 215 N. Main Street, Lockhart 78644, 512-398-2712. Chisholm Trail: www.chisholmtrailbbq.com, 1323 S. Colorado Street, 512-398-6027. Kreuz: www.kreuzmarket.com, 619 N. Colorado Street, 512-398-2361. Smitty's: www.smittysmarket.com, 208 S. Commerce Street, 512-398-9344.

LUCKENBACH DANCE HALL and SALOON

Get down with Willie and Waylon and the Boys. Well, they won't be here, but you can tread in their footsteps and guzzle brewskis where they did.

Hondo Crouch and a couple of friends bought the little town in 1970 and relentlessly promoted it. They held Hug-Ins, Ladies State Chili Busts, Mud Dauber Festivals and daily domino games.

Texas country outlaw singers like Jerry Jeff Walker, Waylon Jennings and Willie Nelson took to it like hungry ticks on a fat dog. In 1973, Jerry Jeff recorded his ¡Viva Terlingua! album here (even though Terlingua is about 500 miles away).

When Willie and Waylon recorded "Luckenbach, Texas" in 1976, a legend was born. But Hondo died the same year.

Willie was a frequent visitor, and back in those days you never knew which musical legend might pop up on the porch to sing. You'll still hear pickers there today. Who knows, maybe they'll be as famous one day. The famous ones you can hear in the concert hall.

What's there to do here when the dance hall isn't holding a concert by a big-name country musician? As the late, great bar mom Marge once said: "It's a bar. You have a beer." Truly immortal words.

FYI: www.luckenbachtexas.com, 412 Luckenbach Town Loop, Fredericksburg 78624, 830-997-3224.

A bust of Hondo Crouch guards the gift shop and saloon of Luckenbach, the Texas town (pop. 3) he put on the map.

Look for many artistic pumpjacks throughout the town of Luling.

Luling
WATERMELON THUMP

OK, where else are they gonna give you a trophy for spitting? A festival celebrating the favorite fruit of summer, the Watermelon Thump has been held here since 1954.

Three separate seed-spitting contests are featured, for children, adults and teams. Think you have the wind to win a trophy? Well, the Thump's current record is 68 feet, 9 1/8 inches, set way back in 1989. (The world record is 75 feet, 2 inches). If it helps you, remember that bounces count.

If you're not up for spitting, try your mouth at the Watermelon Eating Contest, where the idea is to see who can eat one slice of watermelon the fastest. You won't believe how quick some folks are. Ziiiiiiip! and it's gone.

And of course there's a contest for the Champion Watermelon, given to the largest Black Diamond watermelon grown according to specific rules. Top entries get auctioned off. One year, the champ was bought for $22,500.

The Thump features a Watermelon Thump Queen, a carnival, music, food and arts and crafts booths, a car show and a buckin' bull.

Even the town water tower gets into the act: it's shaped and painted like the largest watermelon you ever saw. And check out all that art on the pumpjacks — they're there all year, so you don't have to wait for June to visit Luling.

FYI: www.watermelonthump.com, 421 E. Davis Street, Luling 78648, 830-875-3214. *Note:* Held in late June.

MARBLE FALLS
BLUE BONNET CAFE

Even your dear sainted grandma never made pot roast as melt-in-your-mouth succulent and fork-tender as this. No way, nohow. Plus you get to top your meal off with a pie topped off with mile-high meringue.

It's not illegal to eat at the Blue Bonnet Café without sampling a pie, but it should be. Where else would you find a pie happy hour? Even the doughnuts and cinnamon buns will take your breath away just looking at them. This place will fill you up real good.

Since 1929, first on Main Street and then at its current site on U.S. 281 from 1946, the café has stayed popular. It's expanded a couple of times and is expanding once more. It's always full, and that should tell you something.

Among those who have dined here are George W. and Laura Bush, Lyle Lovett, Richard ("Shaft") Roundtree, Joel Osteen, Willie Nelson and Roger Staubach.

John and Belinda Kemper bought the restaurant in 1981. Belinda is responsible for the famed pies, about 14 different kinds, and she wrote the Blue Bonnet's cookbook.

By the way, contrary to popular belief, the café isn't named after the famed Texas wildflower that's prolific here in the spring — it's named for a lady's hat, or bonnet. That's why it's spelled with two words instead of one.

FYI: www.bluebonnetcafe.net, 211 U.S. 281, Marble Falls 78654, 830-693-2344.

Kathy Hansen (above) tempts with a couple of the Blue Bonnet Cafe's famous pies. The café keeps expanding because people just keep filling up whatever space they have.

Photos by Wyatt McSpadden.

A photo illustration of how the mysterious Marfa Lights sometimes look (top) from the new roadside observation area, with restrooms, east of town.

Marfa
MYSTERY LIGHTS

Sit in the bed of your pickup with a buddy and a beer and tell stories as the eerie lights play. The more you drink, the more lights you will probably see.

Experts have no more an idea about what the lights are than a javelina knows what day of the week it is, but now the state has built an impressive viewing area east of Marfa.

The park has historical markers, a pee place, viewing glasses and a walkway with several plaques detailing the area's natural history.

Look toward the Chinati Mountains across Mitchell Flat; that's where the lights are usually seen. They float, merge and break apart. If you pay attention to the traffic on the highway, you will notice that cars drive by at regular intervals after you see a pair of lights, clearly indicating that some of the lights are some sort of refractions from vehicle lights on the highway behind you. But not all the lights can be accounted for in that fashion ... and, besides, they've been reported here since at least 1883, long before automobiles hit the pavement; indeed, long before pavement.

Some believe they're ball lightning, or atmospheric mirages, or even jackrabbits that have jumped through phosphorus plants. Whatever they are, check 'em out.

FYI: www.marfacc.com/todo/marfalights.php, Marfa Lights Viewing Area is 9 miles east of the city on U.S. 90, 432-729-4942.

Play pool, polish belt buckles with your sweetie and listen to honky-tonk music in the oldest honky-tonk in Texas.

German immigrant Ernst Gruene (pronounced "Green") founded the town in the 1840s, and it was expanded by his son Henry D. in the 1870s. In that expansion was a general store, a gristmill, his mansion and this dance hall and saloon that became the center of the community's social life.

The Depression was a death blow to the town of Gruene, but Gruene Hall survived in what was little more than a ghost town.

In the late 1970s, entrepreneur Pat Molak wandered into town and saw what was possible. He bought up land and started businesses, and before long old Gruene was new again — thriving with new shops, inns and restaurants.

Gruene Hall is now the place where up-and-coming musicians dream of playing; the place where Texas legends like Ray Wylie Hubbard (author of the immortal "Up Against the Wall, Redneck Mother") keep coming back to.

The adjacent Gristmill Restaurant and Bar overlooks the scenic Guadalupe River and has some of the best vittles in all of Texas. If you plan on ordering dessert, go hungry, my friend.

FYI: www.gruenehall.com, 1281 Gruene Road, New Braunfels 78130, 830-606-1281. Gristmill: www.gristmill-restaurant.com, 1287 Gruene Road, 830-625-0684.

Ray Wylie Hubbard, the songwriter who wrote the immortal "Up Against The Wall, Redneck Mother," leans up against the wall at Gruene Hall. Inset: The oldest dance hall in Texas.

Nine-year-old Cody Colvin admires a python.

New Braunfels
SNAKE FARM

The Snake Farm has reptiles of all sorts and colors and sizes. Maybe one is related to your boots.

Opened in 1967, this facility has become a Mecca for generations of snake-lovers who keep returning.

More than 200 species are on display inside, in one of the largest snake displays in North America. You're going to see cobras, black mambas, taipans, prairie rattlesnakes, Massauga snakes, copperheads, rock rattlesnakes, pigmy rattlesnakes, pythons and many more.

In addition to snakes, there's a petting zoo; outdoor cages with lemurs, hyenas, parrots, monkeys, kinkajous and peacocks; and a pond filled with crocodiles and alligators.

Daily animal encounters happen at noon and 3 p.m., with lizard talks and a huge python for photo ops, and on Sunday chicken parts are fed to the crocodilians.

Singer/songwriter Ray Wylie Hubbard paid homage with "Snake Farm," a song about a guy in love with a woman named Ramona who works the counter at the Snake Farm. The engaging sing-along refrain: "Snake Farm — it just sounds nasty. Snake Farm — well, it pretty much is. Snake Farm — it's a reptile house. Snake Farm — Uuuggghhhh."

No road trip is complete without posing under the Snake Farm sign.

FYI: www.exoticanimalworld.com, 5640 I-35, New Braunfels 78132, 830- 608-9270.

Paris
EIFFEL TOWER

Bonjour, y'all. Texas' 65-foot-tall Eiffel Tower was built by the Boiler Makers Local 902 in 1993. No elevator will take you to the top, and you'll see signs warning you not to climb it. The signs are in English and Spanish but, oddly, not in French. *Merde.*

Yeah, everyone instantly recognizes the metal asparagus that is the original 984-foot Eiffel Tower; it's the largest useless structure in the world. Ours has a purpose, however. It wears a big red cowboy hat just to remind everyone that Texas *is* bigger'n France.

Remarkably, no one is sure how Paris, Texas, got its name. It could have been for that big city in France, but it also might have been for a character in the Iliad.

Yes, you can visit Paris without leaving Texas, just as you can visit other exotic locales without leaving the state. You can go to Athens, Atlanta, Berlin, Cleveland, Ireland, Italy, London, Memphis, Miami, Moscow, Naples, Nazareth, Palestine, Pittsburg, Scotland, Turkey and Washington — all without a passport. You'll also find Bug Tussle, Mutt and Jeff, Cut 'n' Shoot and Tarzan.

By the way, don't miss Paris' Evergreen Cemetery, where you can see a statue of Jesus wearing cowboy boots.

FYI: www.paristexas.com, Jefferson Road at South Collegiate Drive adjacent to Love Civic Center, Paris 75460, 903-784-2501. Evergreen Cemetery, 560 Evergreen Street.

Paris, Texas', own Eiffel Tower. It may be smaller than the one in Paris, France, but ours has a fancy red cowboy hat.

Mark Landrum (inset) will teach you how to carve intricate sand castles along the beach. *Photos by Madonna Kimball.*

Port Aransas
Sand Castle Lessons

Take lessons from the "Port A Sand-Castle Guy" and have fun in the sand. Mark Landrum has been helping people build impressive sand castles on the beach since 1999.

Port Aransas and North Padre Island have some of the best sand for building sand sculptures. Mark has two lesson plans: the Family Plan, for one to 10 people, which lasts 60 to 90 minutes, and the Large-Group Plan, for one to 20, which lasts 120 to 150 minutes.

In both lessons you get to learn about stacking sand and how to carve various towers; then you build a fantastic wizard's castle. In the large group, you learn a few extra tips and tricks.

In just a few minutes, Mark will have you building towers, walls, stairs, arches, balconies and rocky cliffs. He uses palette knives, plastic utensils, dental tools, buckets, brushes and a "Willysphere" that makes round shapes.

"Water is the secret ingredient," he says. Apparently, so is "jiggling," a hands-on process he recommends after every step; it helps bond the water with the sand.

An accountant, Mark took a lesson himself in 1999 and got hooked. The Amazin' Walter, who gives lessons on South Padre, said Mark should give lessons, too, so he swapped his spreadsheets for sand castles full-time. He also sells an illustrated lesson book with tools.

FYI: www.sandrum.com, 361-2090-0414.

PORT ARANSAS
SHORTY'S PLACE

Open since 1946, Shorty's is the "Oldest and Friendliest" bar in Port A. That's what the sign says on this small place that's covered in caps and pigs close to the bay.

It's still owned and operated by the same family.

Gladys "Shorty" Fowler was murdered in 1978; her daughter, Miss Rose Smithey, ran it until she died in 2011. Rose's daughter Joy George now runs the place.

One of the effects of alcohol is to make English your second language, but you'll be still able to mumble, "What the ...," when you look around. You'll see a ceiling covered in gimme caps dating back to 1982. You won't even be able to tell what color that ceiling is, the caps are so thick.

Several shelves on one wall are full of pig figurines and toys. When Miss Rose held annual anniversary parties, she would roast a pig out back and friends would bring pig presents. No one is sure why — Miss Rose didn't like pigs. She didn't want to take them home, so she kept them all here.

The jukebox runs the gamut of country music with a lot of coastal and Western thrown in. The bar serves wine, beer and wine coolers and has two regulation-size pool tables. You'll hear music on the porch during the summer months, featuring local talent and bands you may or may not have heard of. There's never a cover charge.

FYI: 823 Tarpon Street, Port Aransas, 78373, 361-749-8077.

Meaghan Wilhite relaxes at Shorty's Place, under a ceiling full of gimme caps and by a wall of pigs. *Photo by Madonna Kimball.*

Our fast-food nation began at a Pig Stand.

Try to get the kids to speak with reverence while here: Pig Stands were where the drive-in restaurant was invented. They also came up with onion rings and the chicken-fried steak sandwich.

And this is the only one left.

During the 1920s, Pig Stands opened in Dallas, Fort Worth, Houston, San Antonio, Beaumont and other places coast to coast. Specializing in good food with fast service, the Pig Stand chain became very popular, reaching its peak in the 1930s with about 130 Pig Stands, mostly in Texas and California — including Hollywood.

Over the years, the number of locations dwindled down; by 2005, only six remained. Owners came and went, struggling to keep the stands alive, but finally all of them closed except for No. 29. It was saved by one of the Pig Stand's employees, Mary Ann Hill, who began working at the Broadway Pig Stand as a waitress at the age of 18 in 1967. She's still running the show.

Today, most diners get their shakes and burgers inside.

The Pig Sandwich has been a featured item on the Stands' menu since the beginning, and Mary Ann makes sure it's still offered. She even has a huge neon "Pig Sandwich" sign lit up in the dining room.

FYI: www.maryannspigstand.com, 1508 Broadway, San Antonio 78215, 210-222-9923.

Step inside Dick's Classic Garage in San Marcos and it looks like the biggest, brightest, cleanest garage you've ever seen. But what it is is a museum — a museum displaying all those old cars you wish you had owned or never gotten rid of, including the rarest of all rare Tuckers.

The museum displays classic American cars from 1929 to 1959 in several large rooms, along with antique oil and gas pumps. A television on one wall runs old automobile commercials like one touting the Edsel's "Teletouch Drive."

The museum opened in 2009, featuring restored vehicles from the collection of founder Dick Burdick.

The collection now includes about 300 vehicles; about 80 are on display at any one time. They're rotated every quarter so you can keep going back to find something new.

Roam around listening to music from the '50s and you'll see a 1931 Avalon Boat Tail Speedster, a '29 Ford Speedster with the rumble seat, a gorgeous '39 Chrysler Imperial Parade Phaeton and several Duesenbergs, including one custom built for gangster Matt Kolb who was killed by rival Al Capone.

The crown jewel of the collection is the 1948 Tucker, one of only 51 ever made and the last one ever built. It has just five-tenths of a mile on the odometer.

FYI: www.dicksclassicgarage.org, 120 Stagecoach Trail, San Marcos 78666, 512-878-2406.

Dick's Classic Garage is full of beautifully restored automobiles, including a rare Tucker (bottom). *Photos by Madonna Kimball.*

Tubing down the scenic San Marcos is one of the best ways to keep cool on a hot summer day in Texas.

SAN MARCOS
TOOBING

It's Texas. It's summer. It's hot. What to do? Get in the water and cool off.

One of the state's most popular family recreation areas is on the San Marcos River — it's exceptionally clear and a cool 72 degrees all year long. Get an inner tube, or "toob," as it's usually written around here, plop your butt in, relax and float downstream. Don't have a toob of your own? Rent one.

Here's the deal: You go to the Lions' rental facility in City Park, get outfitted with a happily yellow toob and any other items you might need — snacks, water, waterproof cases, river shoes, T-shirts, sunglasses, coolers, koozies, waterproof cameras, goggles, water pistols, hats, sunscreen, ice, water bottles, lip balm, swim fins.

Walk down to the river, drop in the water and take a leisurely float for the next hour or so on the most beautiful river in Texas. After you drop over Rio Vista Dam, hop aboard the shuttle bus and ride back to your car. One price lets you do that over and over, all day long.

And don't worry about droughts. Other rivers wither during dry spells, but not this section of the San Marcos. Rising as it does from springs fed by the Edwards Aquifer, the San Marcos River provides a reliable flow of water and would probably be the last river in the area ever to run dry.

FYI: www.tubesanmarcos.com, 170 Bobcat Drive in City Park, San Marcos 78666, 512-396-5466.

You'll be a hero to Bubba Junior when you take him here. Just watch his eyes light up.

You see, the U-Drop Inn was the inspiration for Ramone's body shop in Radiator Springs in the movie *Cars,* and it's easily recognizable as such.

And you probably thought *Cars* was just some cartoon instead of history. While you're at it, remember Cadillac Ranch (see page 13) on the highway west of here? The mountains in Radiator Springs look just like those tail fins.

The U-Drop Inn café and Tower Station were built in 1936 in Shamrock along historic Route 66, the legendary Chicago-to-Los Angeles highway that has inspired songs, TV shows and road trips. The building is now owned by the city.

The unusual building was allegedly inspired by the image of a nail stuck in dirt. It features two flared towers with geometric detailing, curvilinear massing (whatever that means), glazed ceramic tile walls and neon light accents.

It's considered an excellent example of the art-deco style. Deco design this elaborate was more common in large commercial and public buildings; its use in a gas station and café makes the building a real landmark.

The building houses a museum, visitor center, gift shop and the Shamrock Chamber of Commerce office.

FYI: www.shamrocktexas.net, 101 E. 12th Street, Shamrock 79079, 806-256-2501.

Once an art-deco masterpiece, the U-Drop Inn is now a regional visitor center and museum. Mater, Lightning McQueen, and Ramone are nowhere to be seen, however.

Shiner beer bottles rattle down the assembly line after being filled (top). Cereals, malts and artesian waters are aged and blended in pristine copper cookers (bottom).

Shiner
SPOETZL BREWERY

Watch Shiner Bock being made. Now, that's beervana.

The Shiner Brewing Association was started up in 1909 by Czech immigrants here; in 1914, brewmaster Kosmos Spoetzl took over and gave them what would become a legendary Bavarian beer.

Shiner Bock is still Spoetzl's best known and most popular beer, and you'll hear the name being uttered with bravado in icehouses and saloons all across the state. But that's not all Spoetzl makes.

Some of the brews include Shiner Blonde, Black Lager, Hefeweizen, Oktoberfest and the Wild Hare Pale Ale. Be warned: These aren't wimpy light beers consumed by commoners; these are full-bodied, full-flavored yet remarkably drinkable beers favored by redneck royalty.

What's remarkable about the oldest brewery in Texas is that they make every drop of each Shiner beer right here.

Go ahead, take a tour. They use all natural ingredients, and it takes 25 to 28 days from start-up to bottle.

"We don't cut no damn corners," says brewmaster Jimmy Mauric.

And you get free samples of beer at the end of the tour.

Beer may have been invented in Persia around 7000 BC, but it was perfected in Shiner in 1914.

FYI: www.shiner.com, 603 E. Brewery Street, Shiner 77984, 361-594-4294.

Chili is the official State Dish of Texas, and every November a champion is crowned in the birthplace of chili cook-offs.

You don't have to compete. Just go to taste chili made with God-knows-what fixin's, drink beer, watch wet-T-shirt contests and be serenaded off-key.

Aficionados point out that chili is a meat dish; that it has no onions nor, God forbid, beans. Those would make it stew. So forget that Cincinnati stuff.

The first-ever chili cook-off took place in 1967 in Terlingua as a joke between two newspaper columnists, Wick Fowler in Dallas and H. Allen Smith in New York. Each claimed to make the best pot of chili.

A friendly competition was arranged by Frank X. Tolbert on desolate desert property recommended by race-car legend Carroll Shelby. That first competition was declared a draw, but the publicity it garnered meant a real cook-off had to be held the next year, and the next, and the next …

The Chili Appreciation Society International cook-off is held at Rancho CASI de los Chisos on the north side of FM 170, 11 miles west of Study Butte. For years there's been a rival "Original" cook-off, claiming to be heir to the Tolbert-Fowler championship. It's held about four miles from Study Butte on the south side of FM 170.

FYI: www.chili.org, www.abowlofred.com.

Buzzard's-eye view of the Terlingua "Original" Tolbert chili cook-off (top), where cooks stir up bowls of red.

The Porch at Terlingua Ghost Town early in the morning, before the tourists and locals arrive to make it one of the liveliest gathering places in Big Bend (top). In late afternoon, porch denizens ponder this view of the Chisos Mountains as they face east waiting for the sunset to light up Casa Grande peak and the Window formation way off in the national park.

Join the locals on the porch bench as they consume mass quantities of beer and watch the sun go down in the east. Honest. And Dr. Doug will heal what's buggin' you.

Once home to more than 2,000 people, Terlingua is a ghost town today, but it can get real busy on holidays and during cooler months. That's when the porch bench between the Terlingua Trading Company and the Starlight Theatre restaurant fills up.

Sometimes you'll be serenaded by a local guitar-picker, sometimes you'll hear tall tales. On New Year's Day, don't miss the annual Black-Eyed Pea Off and Chicken Bingo.

Rest a while on the bench while the sun sets and you'll see why everyone is facing east. When the light is just right, it will illuminate the Chisos Mountains in reds or golds. And a full silvery moon rising over the peaks will astound you.

Once a thriving mining area for cinnabar — the stuff they make mercury out of — the mines have since died out.

Don't look for a Starbucks, a Dairy Queen or even a Chili's out here. But you will find the Starlight, an old movie theater from the mining heyday. It's the best eatery within 300 miles, with a truly fun and funky atmosphere.

FYI: Terlingua Ghost Town: www.drdougs.com, www.historic-terlingua.com, www.ghosttowntexas.com, www.terlinguacitylimits.com. Starlight Theatre Restaurant & Bar: 631 Ivey Road, Terlingua 79852, 432-371-2326.

Uncertain
Caddo Lake

First off, ain't Uncertain a great name for a town? Second, Caddo Lake is surrounded by one of the largest cypress forests in the world, with trees as old as 400 years. It's home to 250 species of birds and 71 species of fish.

Getting here is half the fun, driving on back roads through forests thick with tall pines. Caddo Lake State Park has a large pavilion, nice cabins for rent, a boat ramp, a lighted fishing pier and nature trails through the thick woods.

The lake is a maze of 26,800 acres of interconnected bayous, channels, cypress thickets and sloughs. Get up early for dawn on the lake and you'll believe there are dragons in the early-morning mists. Oh, wait ... are those gators?

If you're hungry, stop at the Big Pines Lodge. They have great food, a great view and alligators encased in cement on the patio. Don't miss out on the all-you-can-eat frog legs, buckets of beer, jalapeño hushpuppies and fried gator.

If want you an up-close-and-personal tour of the lake, contact John Winn, who was born and raised here. He's proud of the fact that he hasn't lost a tourist to an alligator yet.

FYI: Caddo Lake State Park: www.tpwd.state.tx.us/state-parks/caddo-lake, 245 Park Road 2, Karnack 75661, 903-679-3351. Caddo Outback Backwater Tours: www.caddolaketours.com, 1869 Pine Island Road, 903-789-3384. Big Pines Lodge: www.bigpineslodge.com, 747 Pine Island Road, 903-679-3655.

The spooky view from Campsite 64 at Caddo Lake State Park.

This table and chair at Chuy's restaurant are reserved for John Madden, who drops in every now and then.

Van Horn
ALL MADDEN HAUL OF FAME

Youngsters don't know who John Madden really was, and that's a shame. After he won a Super Bowl as head coach of the Oakland Raiders, he went on to become the greatest sportscaster of all time, because when you're watching Monday Night Football in a beer-induced fog, you absolutely need an authority figure to state the obvious over and over again. Plus he's in the Pro Football Hall of Fame.

Madden hated flying, so he traveled to all those games in an RV. And in 1987, he made a stop at Chuy's Restaurant in Van Horn, just off I-10. Their Mexican food tickled his tonsils, and he kept returning. He set up his "All Madden Haul of Fame" here in the 1990s.

Today, most people know Madden as the man whose name has been on the football video game since 1988. It's sold more than 95 million copies.

Walk inside Chuy's and you're overwhelmed with sports stuff — jerseys, pennants, caps, stickers, framed photographs ... even the TV is tuned to ESPN.

Neon beer signs, an aquarium and a John Wayne cutout figure in one corner are the only non-sports items here.

The lobby has lots of photos of people who've eaten here, including Vanna White and Pat Sajak, Dwight Yoakam, Johnny Cash, Michael Bolton, Ray Price and Clint Black.

FYI: www.chuys1959.com, 1200 W. Broadway, Van Horn 79855, 432-283-2066.

Pay your respects to the second-greatest drink ever invented — after beer, of course. Buy a sample in the old-fashioned soda fountain, but bring your own peanuts.

Dr Pepper was created in 1885 at a Waco drugstore. Pharmacist Charles Alderton served carbonated drinks at the soda fountain, and one day he mixed several fruit syrups together to make a new drink. Everyone loved it.

Popularity spread around Waco, then around Texas, and the new drink was christened "Dr Pepper," but no one really knows where the name came from. At the 1904 St. Louis World Exposition, it became the first major soft drink sold nationwide, followed by Coke and then Pepsi.

Exhibits here take you back in time to the very early years, starting off with the Old Corner Drug Store, where you can talk with Dr. Alderton himself. Well, it's a robot, but he'll still fascinate the young'uns.

Other exhibits showcase early bottling equipment and examples of the earliest Dr Pepper bottles. You'll even find a history of all soft drinks right here.

On the second floor, you are greeted by the sound of commercials and the sight of a 1924 Dr Pepper delivery truck at a re-created 1930s rural general store.

FYI: www.drpeppermuseum.com, 300 S. Fifth Street, Waco 76701, 254-757-1025.

Listen to an animatronic Doc Charles Alderton, inventor of Dr Pepper, at the Dr Pepper Museum.

Ornate carvings around the Ellis County
Courthouse fit Waxahacie's reputation as
Texas' top "Gingerbread City." Legend says that the sculptor
carved his girlfriend's likeness into the stone, but his carvings
got uglier and uglier when his love went unrequited.

ELLIS COUNTY COURTHOUSE

This is one of the grandest courthouses in all of Texas, and it has a fascinating history carved into its walls.

It was built in 1895 of red sandstone and pink granite in a Romanesque style. Theodore Beilharz and a group of talented German stone carvers created the masterpiece.

This courthouse replaced a plain wooden one, so you'd think people would have been happy, but construction was fraught with legal problems. Today it's still controversial.

Get a shop owner on the square to tell you the story about sculptor Harry Herley, who carved the froo-frah decorations on the courthouse. It seems Herley fell in love with Mabel Frame, the daughter of the owner of the boarding house where he stayed. Smitten, he carved her likeness over one of the courthouse entrances. But as Mabel spurned his interest, the embittered Herley's subsequent carvings showed Mabel as uglier and uglier, so the story goes: You can follow Herley's evolving disinfatuation by walking around the courthouse.

Herley apparently even carved Mabel's hoo-ha in stone. It's still there, Bubba. Look for it. Pretty amazing.

Experts say it's all in the imagination of people looking up at the carvings; that the faces are those of traditional European figures. You decide.

FYI: www.waxahachiechamber.com, 101 W. Main Street, Waxahachie 75165, 972-937-2390.

Bonus Trips
I CAN'T BELIEVE I DROVE DOWN THAT ROAD

Head on down these bleak roads and brag to your buddies that you can take on anything.

• **Drink Lots of Coffee.** You need to be sufficiently caffeinated before heading south on U.S. 77 from Sarita to Raymondville. The highway parallels the coast, but the water is far enough away that you don't get to see any of it. You won't see much more than pavement, either. You know you're in for a boring drive when you see a sign warning that you won't find another gas station for at least an hour. Gas up, Bubba. Out here ranches are measured in MPG — miles per gate.

• **Desolation Highway.** Farm Road 2810 from Marfa to Ruidosa — also known as the Pinto Canyon Road — is barren and beautiful, but more than a little intimidating, especially after you read the hand-lettered warning sign. You're unlikely to see another vehicle for the entire 60 miles. The south portion of the road, about 22 miles, is nasty gravel. It's as hot as the Devil's armpit, and even the lizards carry canteens. The only thing out here is Chinati Hot Springs — an easy-to-miss but welcome oasis in the middle of this desolation.

• **Pump Jacks and Peanuts.** Take U.S. 385 from Seminole (the peanut capital of Texas) to Andrews, and all you'll see over this flat ground are peanut farms and oil pumps. Finding something of interest on this drive is about as easy as pushing a noodle through a keyhole.

A clear warning that some people really don't want you to drive down the Pinto Canyon Road.

The Dom rock still stands to the east of the parking lot at Big Hill on the River Road, the most scenic drive in Texas.

Bonus Trips
I'm So Glad I Drove Down That Road

Now these are drives you can really enjoy.

• **Don't Dig Up Dom:** Farm Road 170 (the River Road) from Lajitas to Presidio is the most scenic drive in Texas, with the river, mountains and hoodoos galore. Don't hit the mountain goats. At Big Hill — don't worry, you'll know it; it's big — look upstream for a great view of the Rio Grande to see how imaginary the border between the U.S. and Mexico really is. Nearby is the Dom rock and Kevin Costner Point — featured in the early Costner flick *Fandango*, in which a group of UT frat buddies go on a road trip to dig up something or someone named Dom on the banks of the Rio Grande. And don't miss Fort Leaton, a restored trading post near Presidio that has a particularly bloody history.

• **The Real Gulf Coast:** Texas Highway 35 from Aransas Pass to Palacios is the unpretentious Gulf Coast. You'll go by beaches, boats and fishing piers — don't miss the two-mile-long Copano Bay Fishing Pier — windswept giant oaks and the famed Hu Dat restaurant near Fulton.

• **The Real Hill Country:** Go ahead on down Ranch Road 337 from Medina to Campwood. This is easily one of the most scenic drives in all of Texas, second only to Farm Road 170 in the Big Bend. It's what the real Hill Country looks like, all twisty roads and steep hills. Maple trees line much of the road; when they turn red and yellow in the fall, it's magic. You're also likely to see lots of exotic game on the ranches.

ABOUT THE AUTHOR

Author Allan C. Kimball wasn't born in Texas, but, as the bumper sticker says, he got here as soon as he could. He was even baptized a Texan in the Brazos River.

This is his sixth travel book about Texas. He is also the author of two historical novels set in the Big Bend of West Texas and is a member of the Western Writers of America.

Allan is an award-winning journalist and photographer with a long career as a reporter and editor at daily newspapers in Texas. Over the years he has interviewed several presidents, discovered clandestine government airstrips and covered stories as diverse as chili cook-offs and prison boot camps, from disastrous tornadoes to sea turtle rehabilitation, from gubernatorial races to beer-drinking goats. As a member of the Baseball Writers Association of America, he covered the Houston Astros and Major League Baseball for several years. And he has chased killer bees throughout Central and South America. His articles have appeared in many national magazines.

He and his wife Madonna live in Wimberley, Texas.